SCHIRMER'S LIBRARY
OF MUSICAL CLASSICS

Vol. 2084

WOLFGANG AMADEUS MOZART
EINE KLEINE NACHTMUSIK

Piano, Four Hands

To access companion recorded audio online, visit:
www.halleonard.com/mylibrary

Enter Code
3595-7465-1802-7153

Audio features performances and play-along tracks of primo part only and secondo part only.

Pianists on the recordings:
Wilanna Kalkhof, primo part and **Stefanie Jacob, secondo part**

ISBN 978-1-4234-8552-0

G. SCHIRMER, *Inc.*

DISTRIBUTED BY
Hal•Leonard®

Visit Hal Leonard Online at
www.halleonard.com

World headquarters, contact:
Hal Leonard
7777 West Bluemound Road
Milwaukee, WI 53213
Email: info@halleonard.com

In Europe, contact:
Hal Leonard Europe Limited
42 Wigmore Street
Marylebone, London, W1U 2RY
Email: info@halleonardeurope.com

In Australia, contact:
Hal Leonard Australia Pty. Ltd.
4 Lentara Court
Cheltenham, Victoria, 3192 Australia
Email: info@halleonard.com.au

Eine kleine Nachtmusik

Wolfgang Amadeus Mozart (K.525)

Secondo

Eine kleine Nachtmusik

Wolfgang Amadeus Mozart (K.525)

Printed in the U.S.A.

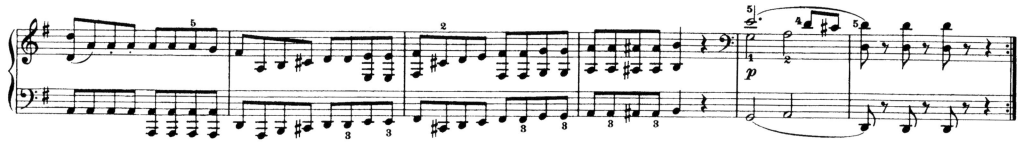

*This repeat has been omitted on the recording.

*This repeat has been omitted on the recording.

Romanze.
Andante.

Menuetto.
Allegretto.

A

Fine.

B Trio.

C

Menuetto da capo.

Menuetto.
Allegretto.

Fine.

Menuetto da capo.

Rondo.
Allegro.

Rondo.
Allegro.

A

*This repeat has been omitted on the recording.

*This repeat has been omitted on the recording.

*This repeat has been omitted on the recording.

*This repeat has been omitted on the recording.

Coda.